ANOTHER CROSSING

Acknowledgements

I would like to acknowledge and give thanks to the Creator for guiding me to write poems that root family and friends in the history of the city of Leeds and the African Diaspora.

To my mother, father, for the gift of life, to my grandmother and grandfather, whose journey to England gave me the substance to stitch stories tightly together. To my aunties Dana and Dahlia, to my uncles Desmond and Pops and my auntie Blossom McLaren for their shared stories of family ties, love and separation. To my brothers and sisters, my children, Jadey, Rheima and Ali, whose unconditional love keeps me going, keeps me smiling and laughing. To my new grandson, Eli Ibrahiim. Also to Jeremy Poynting and staff at Peepal Tree Press – Hannah Bannister, Dorothea Smartt, Kadija George and Adam Lowe for their encouragement and support to write this collection. To Paulette Morris, Oluseyi Ogunjobi, Fosuwa Andoh, Lisa Blanchette, Anita Wisdom, Ugochi, Tracy Fishley, David Hamilton, Joe Williams, Sandra Whyles and Cordelia and Nicola Francis for keeping me grounded with the truth and loving friendship which is priceless. One love! Jah blessings! Many thanks to the El Gouna Egypt (Writers Residential and Retreat) and to the Arvon Foundation, Hebden Bridge, for time spent in a wonderful and peaceful space.

KHADIJAH IBRAHIIM

ANOTHER CROSSING

PEEPAL TREE

First published in Great Britain in 2014
Peepal Tree Press Ltd
17 King's Avenue
Leeds LS6 1QS
England

ISBN13: 9781845232412

Supported using public funding by
ARTS COUNCIL
ENGLAND

Dedicated to the loving memory of
Trevor and Lucilda Wynter,
Elisha and Eugenie McLaren,
and to the spirit of my ancestors
who allow my very being to exist.

CONTENTS

PROLOGUE

AFRO-WEARING BROTHAS & SISTAHS
(1970s)

Calling all
Afro-wearing
brothas and sistahs

Remember how the 1970s made us ride
on a conscious vibe?
Afros were picked way high
like Angela Davis's Black Power fist

Afros were antennas in the sky
connecting history's bloodline
tangled through triangle trade-lines

Old man river don't cry for me
We'll be forever loving Jah

Jah elevated a new NATION
now declaring we're here to stay in Britain
where Afro-wearing people

heard the call
Let freedom ring
By any means necessary

Calling all
Afro-wearing,
brothas and sistahs

Calling all
funkadelic
soul conscious,
get down on it people

Calling all righteous
and understanding people…

What!
Hold-on… Wait a minute…
OVERS…
OVERstanding,
roots and culture
natty dread-wearing
brothas and sistahs

Calling all
pimps and pimped out
street hookers,
and mothers and fathers
and mothers whose babies
got no fathers
because of the System,
the pressure the Eurocentric ideals
that's got brothas
crawling between prison walls,
pumped up on being the lesser,
down, down, down in life
asking, dear God,

Where is the love?

Calling brothas and sistas
who stand long
on Garvey's dream
sing Robert Nestor Marley

Kinky reggae
Kinky reggae now

Remember the Man Shaft

Shut yah mouth… you damn right

Remember his smooth
ebony body,
his high sheen

Afro,
he was groomed
in *all* the right places
He just had some sistahs wanting
…just got this sistah thinking…

Calling all brothas and Idrins
who turned kung fu kicks
in cobbled back streets
allegiant to the Panthers,
the Brotherhood, living the struggle

while politicians held National Front positions,
teachers taught Columbus
preached straight-hair Jesus,
believing WE did not know

WE,
in tune with
all Afro-wearing
brothas and sistahs
who fought for our freedom and rights

That's why I'm calling
…and I'm calling and I'm still calling
and why the hell not?

Isn't this an
Afro wearing
time we live in

or what?

A SNAPSHOT HISTORY OF LEEDS

56 COWPER STREET

56 COWPER STREET

As Grandma said,
New broom sweeps clean
but the old one knows all the corners,
so brick by brick
I rebuild a house that once stood in Chapeltown,
56 Cowper Street,
a Victorian terrace with a green front door,
my grandparent's home,
where I slid down the staircase banister
into laughter and now into memory.

I try to remember all things special,
like the Canadian gift of an oil-painted portrait
of my dad and Aunt Sylvia
hanging against midnight-blue
circle-print wallpaper in the lounge;
Grandma's rose-porcelain tea sets;
her crystal and dust-free silverware –
for viewing only.

This seven-bedroom house signified
Importance in the ready hands of my
Jamaican family, blood spiced with Africa
and something of the colonial past.

Grandma grew roses and dahlias
in the front garden, picked gooseberries
to make jam and wine; Grandad dug tuff dirt
in the back yard, planted potatoes and cabbage.
Their tea they sipped from ceramic mugs,
blue for Grandad, red for Grandma,
except on special occasions, when Granny liked
a teacup with a saucer.

Every day, full-cooked breakfast from the kitchen –
nutmeg-spiced condensed milk,
smooth cornmeal porridge,
salt fish and callaloo, fried dumplings –
filled hungry bellies;
and the ritual of meals
at the oak dining-room table
with family and familiar friends,
each with a story
from which lessons were to be learnt,
now brings smiles.

GRANDMA

18

HOMESPUN

My stays at Cowper Street were long –
sometimes up to a year of Grandma's "kidnap" –
to compensate for my father being overseas,
so I was split between
my mother's looser apron strings
and Grandma's homespun rules
of do's and don'ts and decency,
when chores were regular and never shirked
for skipping ropes, jacks and hot rice,
when skylarking carried the repercussion of:
Stand up straight, pull your socks up!
Never mind playing outside wid dem pickney.
Dem favour leggo beast.
Go find a book and read.
At Cowper Street,
love's strict hand nurtured studies,
mental arithmetic and recitation on the spot,
but Grandma also styled party frocks
on the Singer in her bedroom
and quilted the foundations of our kinship
for generations; told me of her great-grandfather Quashie
and her Welsh-East Indian grandfather, Jabez,
who gambled away the family's Jamaican land,
and of her first and second husbands,
her six children: five names beginning with the letter 'D',
the first born with an 'S';
these stories stitched tightly to me.

HOME SCHOOLED

In my aunties' bedroom, the world moved
to the heartbeat of *I'm black and I'm proud*.
Aunty Dana and Dahlia wore natural hairstyles
cut pepper-grain short, Afro-picked, combed smooth;
their stereo played
soul melodies of Curtis Mayfield
We got to have peace,
and the reggae revolution of Steel Pulse
stirred their words.
Their bedroom walls carried
posters of Garvey, Ras Daniel Heartman's natty roots children,
and the Jackson Five, with their doctorates in Afros.

Combing through the thickness
of my little girl plaits, Aunty Dahlia tied satin ribbons,
left them long to dangle at my neck.
Aunty Dana spoke of ancestry,
African empires before Hawkins sailed in greed,
gave me the gift of their narratives
and books for my birthdays –
on Harriet Tubman and her soldier stance –
books not seen in schools.
They educated me.

GRANDAD'S HOME BREW

In the front room, whether indigo skies
or a rainy grey covered the afternoons,
Grandad hammered metal caps
onto brown glass bottles of homemade brew,
as he listened to Beethoven's symphonies,
or sang folk songs with mento rhythms
like *River bank Coverly, River to the bank Coverly...*
paced to match the speed of his work.

The taste of beer already bottled
would wet the mouths of Will Ruddock,
Valentine and Winifred Daley
who synchronised visits to slam dominoes
to wood, and fire up games of Ludo.
And more big people brought talk,
not always for a child to hear,
their tongues navigating the West Indies,
stretching back to Paul Bogle's Stony Gut revolt.

And within this room in Cowper Street
Grandad rallied the Brotherhood
like a rebel god, hungry to put
wrongs to right, reshape man's thinking.

THE ATTIC IS SILENT PLACE

"We speak to you by parables, but would willingly bring you to the
right, simple, easy, and ingenuous exposition, understanding,
declaration, and knowledge of all secrets."

Each room at Grandma's house
had its own story with secrets
concealed in sky-high ceilings,
covings and walls,
like the attic room on the 2nd floor
where the door was rarely opened,
if at all.

Steps snaked up to the attic
where cobwebs hung, and nobody
ever talked about going there –
unlike the three-room basement,
another dark place of damp and cold
with a kitchen range aged with time
and an old pine door, repaired
with bent-up nails, that creaked.

The basement led to the back yard where
washing was hung and soil dug hard
like back home in Jamaica,
a sprawling gooseberry bush hugged the wall
and berries were picked for wine 'n jam treats.
But way up in the attic, darkness stood still –
and dusty rails and door handles
were a sign not to enter.

It took a curious mind, an adventurous
soul – or a fass child whose ears
too hard – who couldn't resist discovering

another den for Samantha, Wayne and I
to play in during school holidays.

The attic was a silent place, with a single
dim bulb that added to the mystery.
A flick of the switch and an Aladdin's
cave was found, four rooms filled with junk,
all kinds of things: used chemistry sets –
from Uncle Douglas –
old boxes with family names,
and other things not quite belonging,
things you couldn't place –
like the room next to the stairs.

It smelled earthy, musty, a place
that invited no questions, just acceptance.
In it stood a table covered with a white cloth
clean as the day, a red one too.
Candles dressed the table as if an altar
in St Augustine's church where I gave out hymnbooks,
and next to it was a robe or apron,
its use mysterious, for at the age of seven –
too shy to ask questions,
since I would have to admit to being nosey –
I had to keep the secret of what I'd seen.

Thirty years and more, with 56 Cowper St
demolished a time ago by
Chapeltown's cries for modernisation,
(re-gentrification from beneath our feet),
and with Grandma's ashes scattered and
Grandad then living at Roxholme Grove,
these childhood adventures
were a sepia thought at the back of my mind,
until I met an elder,
a Jamaican-born woman,

who, after introductions and smiles
and a kind exchange of words,
revealed her links to my grandparents,
mentioned her Rosicrucian faith,
and at that moment the attic room
at Cowper Street came back and
I began to imagine its purpose –
to seek self-knowing –
as a secret to be kept, better not revealed.

In big people talk the mystery of things
never leaves you, until they are made clear.

KHADIJAH AND HER FATHER, GATHORNE MOUNT

4, GATHORNE MOUNT

At 4 Gathorne Mount, our house,
mine when Grandma released the reins,
cooking pots crowned the stove-top daily,
smells of Mum peeling back skin from onions,
grating fresh ginger, mixing spices to season-up meat,
life moved with a looser reggae beat.

It was five a we giggling pickney
who loved to ramp and play:
Andrew, Leroy, Angela, me –
and late-born Damian.
We never knew when time came
fi settle down like a pot of kidney beans
in wait for bay leaf, thyme and coconut cream.
Mum always said: *Unoo favour heng pon nail,*
and: *Who caan't hear must feel*
– and we did.

As often as we could, we escaped outside
through cobbled backstreets
that led down to the beck, for games
of British bulldog and hot rice.
We'd speed across the beck,
chased by dogs named Rex and Shep
just to get to Bankside street, to Joof's,
Freda's and Freddy's house.
We kids scraped knees, bled cuts to tears,
as regular as the news of the day
heard over gardens walls and washing lines
of who was doing what in marital affairs.

Back home, scuffed shoes and black pumps
kicked off, after a supper of Milo and toast,
we'd huddle beside the kitchen gas fire

to view a picture palette of only three stations
on our rental Rumbelow TV.
We liked how Black kept on the attack
in *Love Thy Neighbour*,
but *Black and White Minstrels*,
and Jim Davidson's "Chalky",
with thick lips and big nose jokes,
were never found funny in our home.

When Sundays came, there was no choice
for Angela and me. We had to
go to church with Mother Brown's twins,
Jackie and Janet and Miss Tiny's (Mummy T.)
grandaughter, Dionne, in our Sunday best,
memorise Hail Mary, pray for forgiveness,
go to confession, light candles for God's joy.
Ours came from the incense
of rice and peas and chicken at home.
("Fresh" chicken came from African George Yam shop –
"fresh" later discovered to mean live,
kept in the back of the shop.)
Sunday's were also for dusting off
the smoked glass coffee table,
Lynch's Spanish Tina reproduction
and the lava lamp in the front room,
as we listened to Desmond Decker,
Jimmy Cliff and Millie Small,
flip sides and dub versions by U Roy and Big Youth
on the Blue Spot radiogram;
later the soul train of Isaac Hayes,
Al Green, Gladys Knight,
Millie Jackson's *Caught Up*
and Dorothy Moore's *Misty Blue*
on the new stereo.
That's when we pickney learnt to dance.

Sometimes Mum held a Blues in the cellar
where ravers came to rub-a-dub
under the Babycham-box lampshade,
drink white rum, mannish water,
eat pattie and curry goat.
As mothers do – she knew her children –
she catch us from di corner of her eye,
and rush us back to bed
wid rum cake, a snowball and babycham
to share between us all,
because this is big people story…
But ah fass, so I hide, all for a glance
of folk entering our house.

Our house carried full volumes of visitors,
like Sweets and Icilyn, Cushy-Peck, Fitzy,
Red-skin Danny and Moonfoot,
and reggae bands like an album collection
stacked and spun from Sir Yanks record shop:
Jimmy Cliff would stay the night,
dating my godmother Peggy,
the Cimarons, too, singing
'On the Rock' 'n 'Routing for a Cause',
and Mummy cooked for Bunny Wailer
at the Electric Press, who later
sent me a postcard of Steve Biko,
with an invite to Jamaica.

It was the days of Green Shield stamp books,
the pop man calling with crates
of dandelion and burdock, and cherryade –
collect pop bottles, and you could make a bob or two
to buy penny and halfpenny sweets:
black jacks and Bazooka Joes,
two-ounces of cop-cops or sherbert lemons,
and *My Guy* magazines for the *real* love stories

and the pin-ups of Blondie and David Bowie,
dreams that stretched the perimeters of the house.

From William Hill's to Dinn's shop,
and down to the Gaiety,
old Gathorne's bricks, now fallen,
remain like keloids on our heart strings,
remind us of a generation
that built better stories than the houses.

HAREHILLS PRIMARY

HAREHILLS MIDDLE SCHOOL

Young hearts shake hands across cultures,
feet masquerade in time to heartbeats;
Lisa, Yasmin and show-off kids like me
danced the bump, played jacks and skipped
in the playground of Harehills Middle School.
But the real boastful kids were those in
Mrs Senior's dance class,
the stars of Grey trophy high jump, long jump,
the netball and football team;
their triumphs at tournaments mapped ideas
of what we could be.

In lessons at old wood desks
with redundant, stained inkwells
(used by Uncle Douglas fifteen years before
when it was still a boys' school),
we read history books about William the Conqueror,
1066, the Tudors and Victorians;
fractions and algebra were never fully grasped,
though Math's classes were slipper strict
in the hands of Mr Adkin.
High-tempered Mr Richmond
of the hairy face taught English,
threw words and pupils round the room.
Miss Taylor taught our hands
to curve, to mould clay pots
– another ashtray to take home.

Sometimes we earned merits for excellence,
more often detention or the cane.

Excitement rippled one morning assembly
when Mr Bramwell was due to announce
who'd won the brand new chopper bike

with a bell and tassels,
but first we had to say the Lord's prayer
and sing *Kumbayah, My Lord, Kumbayah*,
before Colleen Green and her brother Silas
were announced the winners.

Jammed with working-class families
with very little, we kids
stirred crazy to collect old newspapers,
did sponsored runs and walked to a frenzy
to add to the school funds –
all to gain house points
and win the trophy
for Red or Blue, Yellow or Green.

We were happy for halfpenny sweets
in a paper bag, Dainty toffees,
savoury vinegar crisps, Spanish and sherbet fountains
from the school tuck shop;
happy for youth clubs, seven inch vinyl
played on the Bush player with a tin pan sound;
we danced to Abba, Bay City Rollers and Michael Jackson,
wore Afros, flares, crocheted hats and plaits.

Sunday's top twenty on the radio brought anxious
youth to guess who's at number one
– before Thursday's *Top of the Pops*, *Smash Hits*
and *Jackie* magazine.
Remember when Third World's
Now that we found love
What are we gonna do with it?
got to number one?

And when BBC2 came to make
a documentary at the school,
they used the Third World hit

as the theme tune for the show –
Orlando Weekes at home and at school,
a family affair. And when we saw *In the City,*
film of the dance production *Paradise Lost,*
documentary of Harehill's crumpled streets
on our TVs, we saw nothing *then* to regret.
For us kids nothing mattered but
the friends we made and the games we played.

ROOTS ON TV

Oats porridge, hard-dough bread,
a sip of herb tea for breakfast –
I'd remember to wipe my mouth
at the bus stop on Roundhay Road
where I walked short Grace Jones Afro style,
black girl pride channelling my steps.
I rode two buses to Bramley Town End
just to get to school. At Intake High,
during class registration
the teacher asked,
Who watched Roots on TV?
and me, the only black child in class,
screwed up my face,
kissed mih teeth at the classroom laughter,
cut my eye at Janet Whitehouse
sat next to me scribbling NF
on her desk – a white girl pride.

At Intake School not one
hard-dough, bread-eating kid in my class,
just chips and beans.
NF and British Movement followers
propelled spits, taunts in Yorkshire,
slurred names: *Chocolate Drop,*
Nig Nog, Sambo, Jungle Bunny,
Golly Wog, Kunta Kinte, Kizzy go home.

NATTY DREAD PROTEST

(For John "Ruben" Grant)

I

His natty dread brought disturbance
amongst the teachers,
disgusted talk in the staff room
of a youth man, neither turbanned Sikh
nor kippahed Jew,
who wouldn't fit the rules.

He'd been looking for a dream
beyond the dust and bricks of Leeds,
holding a belief in a King of Kings,
an ever-living god.
Stepping hard-core in Clarks' shoes,
fresh on Rastafari reasoning,
reading or hearing a Bible chapter a day,
psalms and Garvey's sermons
recited at Number 72,
he versed ideas from reggae
and niyabinghi drums,
a promise so real you could touch it.
His Afro natty was too tall
for classroom walls,
too wide to fit the door-frame.

Excluded to safeguard the school rules,
too uniformed to bend to his roots'
song of redemption,
he stood ready and waiting,
ready to learn lessons.
Outside the parents call a protest
for their children's right to education.

II

"They shall not make baldness upon their heads…"
— Leviticus 21:5

You mean you remember
di natty protest?
Even I don't remember too much.
I was dread and that was it.
I didn't care for school cos school
didn't care for me.

I was dread, Natty Fari.
With age I learnt
I and I natty was my protest song,
a radical roots demonstration,
I-man own expression
inna mi heart dread vibration.
Look at me now!
No dread to speak of.
Lost my hair real quick to balding.
How di times have changed!
It's funny now, but I guess
back then it meant much more
than what is physically
here on mi head.
Natty forever a living ting
I an I hold inna mi heart.
Seeeeen!

UNION JACK

Mum always said she should have gone back home
when *Rivers of Blood* ran deep
in the current of Enoch Powell's hate
…the Tiber foaming with blood…
an urgent encouragement of re-emigration…

Send them back; load the ship with
chocolate smiles, send them back
before blacks take the whip hand…

No Blacks, no dogs, no Irish!
One down, a million to go!

But unoo barn hyah, Mum said.
I sweep the Union Jack
under the bed.

YOUTH RAGE 1975: WARRIOR CHARGE

Remember, remember the 5th of November,
a day to throw yuh ole things in the road,
hold street competitions to build
the biggest bonfire just for boast.

In 1975 Chapeltown lit up
into a riot attack so fierce
the police almost had to surrender.
Parents and leaders rallied to halt

a heavy police presence
come to clash 'n assault.
Fire engines circled
to hose down fires;

the law's boots crept
between foliage in gardens,
and from an undercover CID car
on Spencer Place.

A gust of angry voices flew
from Francis Street, the Granges
and Rossington Grove
as three hundred youths rose up.

Silence erupted into flames
in a warrior charge
fuelled by anger,
the tinder of frustration,

and rehashed tales of Teddy boys
chasing down their fathers.
Heavy on their minds were false arrests
and raids on blues and locals' houses.

Youth battled West Yorkshire police –
it was Beirut in Leeds, cuss up and screams.
Not even Maureen Baker's prayers
could stop the clash of race 'n hate.

Black Mariah at the ready,
a convoy come slow 'n menacing,
swinging truncheons,
dogs at dem side.

Youth dem at the ready,
broken bricks at dem side,
bonfire debris stacked n' brandish
as the artillery.

In the heat of stone beats and cussing,
a CID car torched, no local car touch,
not a scratch or a dent.
But Mr Morris di local

steelpan player coming home
from work in his van,
was snatched and arrested,
not a word to him wife.

Twelve youths arrested,
some taken outta school,
on essay confession.
Mrs Paul, Head from Elmhurst,

bring black lawyers from London
most freed, four serve sentence.
What a day, what a night,
what a tribulation!

YOUTH RAGE 1981

We never imagined
it would happen again, the night
rage burnt cars and shops,
rioting a stone's throw from my house.

Six years later, big youth,
man and woman,
raged up a passion,
set out the streets like an arena
for a bull fight with the Babylon.
Fire! Fire! Disturbed hearts smashed
bricks through the smoky heat,
exploded against discrimination,
suss laws and racist attacks,
and inner city streets burnt to ash,
because there was 'f' all else to do
but sign on, get your UB40,
passport to collect the dole.

ROCK AGAINST RACISM

In our back-to-back and through-terraced houses,
working-class black and white
youth played Snap!
Sex Pistols latched onto this white heat,
graffitied Elizabeth's head,
stuck two fingers up, wore safety-pins
and spat on the Union Jack.
We watched them pogo dancing up and down
to The Clash's *white riot* of reggae-snatched rhythms,
while Maggie snatched milk,
brought recession and the poll tax.
And when The Specials rocked against racism,
they marched right past my street
up to Potternewton Park
'til it was *like a zebra crossing, black and white,*
black and white as far as you can see.

BLACK IS BLACK 1980s

Black is black
in we heartbeat of chants
in we music –
mixing soul and gospel
beating bass 'n drum.
You caan't hold us down,
we players of instruments,
we makers of music,
we singers, we dancers –
it's just how we do it.

From front-room parties
to basement raves,
all-dayers, all-nighters,
rare reggae grooves,
James Brown's funk rhythms
that came right back
in the break-beats,
the loops, the mixing down,
house and hip hop
best foot moves –
tearing up the warehouse parties.

We locked and popped
and did the Wop,
corked the Wag Club,
the Gallery and Harveys Wine Bar,
rocked in Doc Marten boots,
Levi 501s, and balanced
flat caps over curly perms and extension plaits.

We moved against Thatcher's time,
flipped the script to come again
in UK street riots.

Talking blues, keep on talking blues
They say your feet is just too big for your shoes...

From the underground,
DJ's called up all the elements:
sound-system dance,
Genesis FM,
Funky Dreads,
Soul 2 Soul,
with a tumping bass,
while Black and British
voice of an angel, Caron Wheeler,
smoothed the heat,
kept us moving
back to life,
back to reality.

We African
we African Caribbean
we Black
we Black and British,
however we want it to be,
we ride pan de riddim
wheel it back pan de version,
sound system styleee... and into the 90s...

There's nothing like this...
Sip a glass of cold champagne wine...
there's nothing like this...

COME WHAT MAY WE'RE HERE 2 STAY
(After Windrush)

We crossed in honour to defend the mother country,
with cocoa, rum and sugar in we skin,
and the milk and honey England never bring.

We kept on moving, the elder heads
marching in exodus against
race, immigration and deportation laws.

Free thinkers composed slogans for pickets:
Come what may we're here to stay -
Without us there is no Britain! Live and let live!

My grandad said we endured this pain too long.
Was it God we were waiting for? – his words
like the hooping of a sermon into song.

Amazing *how sweet the sound*
of his dark-skin pride
of *better must come*.

The decades of cold under we feet,
our children's children barn hyah, we as equal as de next.
"*So give us our money… so we can pay the rent*" –

old chants routed across time.
Even Churchill recalled how we swelled the pot of Capital,
how the West Indies made the Empire rich and strong.

In the aftermath of Hitler's bombs, in a post-war boom
of more jobs than workers, we crossed the ocean
loaded with skills, recrafted and rebuilt dreams.

In a strange land, we made the grass grow green again.
But *man to man is so unjust* and still tangle we blood
in slave-trade wind. *In treating man less than fly,*
to tell the reason why it's so, into history we must go…

MY MOTHER

MY MOTHER'S DUTCH POT OF STORIES

My mother can tell a good story,
the same way she cooks up a meal
that will always sweet you.
The ingredients of her words
will fill your belly with the flavours of life;
you'll taste the tale.

She'll capture a moment in time
with her pots and pans,
take you hand in hand across an ocean,
to a place where hurricanes
are named Charlie and Gilbert,
to her Jamaica before Independence,
before she travel at the age of twenty-two.

In the heat of Saturday soup,
when the mood takes her,
she'll start to talk about back home,
mixing her talk with gestures,
she'll drop a joke or two like boiled dumplings,
make you fall over into belly-busting laughter,
she'll forget a word and you just got to guess,
move through each sentence when she wheel
into patois and say,
"Pass mi di sint'in, pan tappa di ting."

She's a storyteller from the days of old
she don't labba labba up in anyone business –
Oh no!
My mother talks with substance grounded
from a living history – with all the goings-on,
connecting blood ties to family roots,
from her mother, Eugenie,
a higgler woman on the market,

and her father, Elisha, alias Daddy Mac,
a foreman on the Kingston railway,
and member of three lodges.
She'll tell you how she helped Mama
to push the cart to Linstead market,
and balance baskets of goods on her head
to sell in Coronation market.
She'll tell you how the British empire stretch
its neck like mongoose, and how she dress up
in pretty prim and proper frilly-frilly frock,
her knees and teeth shining in the smiles
and waves of red, white and blue flags
for the Queen's jubilee visit to the island;

or when she was little and fas'
how she cut through a barbwire fence
that tore the side of her face;

or when her brothers, Desmond and Pops, use to go uptown,
to catch a big show in a friend's father's funeral car
to rock easy to ska beats and slow-it-down rhythms,
Take Your Time' No Need to Worry,
hit tunes of Hopeton Lewis;

or how she and Knock-knee Pearly from Cuba
knock tins and sing back-up for Ken Boothe, Alton
and Hortense Ellis when they rehearsed
under the mango tree on Fifth Street,
how she grew with Alton before he reach England.

She was born ah country, one of eight children
in Lawrence Tavern in the parish of St Andrew's,
before she come to town,
studied at Trench Town Government School
and turn Kingstonian girl, prim-up
in the homemade fashion of 1957

to go to big big theatres and dances,
from Majestic, Palace, the Ambassador in Trench Town,
Cross Roads to the Carib and Ward Theatres.

Dutty tough, she lived on Fifth Street
(her sister Violet moved to Maxwell Avenue by Jackie Edwards)
amongst the church singers,
hard-time workers, higglers in the markets –
she would say to me and Angela,
Ah wha'ppen to oonoo,
ah Coronation market u deh?
if we didn't sit with knees together
or keep our voices down.

She'll remember the talk in Trench Town
how Mortimo Planno was sent
to Africa to meet the king,
Haile Selassie of Ethiopia.

She'll tell you the tale,
transport you to the place
so you feel you've been there too.
In the folds and layers of the words
she make you come back, hungry for more.

GRANDAD TREVOR

FOLKTALES 'N SONGS
(*For Granddad Trevor*)

Singerman, sing me a song
Singerman, sing me a song

Between stories of way back when,
world politics, Caribbean history,
a song or two, Granddad says he's
ready to open the gates. He said,

"I've been here a long time,
seen walls fall and concrete grow,
I could've gone long-time ago,
but I'm just holding the ground
until my time comes naturally."

As sharp as a needle and to the point
He talk some and leave some –
things long forgotten from the past,
like Bustamente and the common
cause of the people,
of Norman Manley's speech in 1962
at Lancaster House on Independence,
after the voters rejected Federation.

Grandad read the *Gleaner* on Jamaica's
new constitution and quoting Manley said,
"We walked in peace because we were a free
people, always right and forever ready,
long before 1944 when all we Jamaicans
got the right to vote.

"We reach maturity to run our island
long before I left in '57,
and come to the heart of Empire
when its sun set. We people
were ready to step onto the world stage.

"With our Brotherhood from Cowper Street,
we stood on the backs of our ancestors,
knowing our history didn't start on slave ships.
We led our campaigns to clean up Chapeltown,
kept a sense of pride.

"It's not the knock down you get
it's how you get up," he'd say.
"Mrs. Harriett, Mrs.Cruse and
the others knew all that:
we taught Black history;
Grandma and Mrs Davis saved
Studley Grange nursery, and
at the Centre we made space for sound systems
so di youth didn't get left behind.

"We elders watered the branches
so Uhuru could grow in Violet Hendrickson,
Annette Liburd and Imru Caesar, who created
with artistic freedom and no apologies –
legacy of tuff times. We watch the world
mingle and mix our history.

"Winnie Mandela fire the Soweto uprising in '76,
and I live to see the day Mandela spoke
at the Civic Hall when he came to Leeds
to receive the Key, in the place
where freemen of the city meet.
I hear Mpho's poem of a Zulu healing woman,
connecting me to my African heritage."

Watery-eyed, he smiled and said,
"I don't want no church song,
or hymns of Jesus, please!
I don't keep that kind of faith,
and long stop wondering about their God,
though I keep a belief in the Creator.
Give me the folk songs of my time
the ones that I grew up with from Jamaica."
He hums a melody and I search for the words.
He said, "I'm ready, and I know
everything I should, done what I can,
can't walk down the garden path no more;
I walked my garden more times
than you know, dug it deep,
turned soil so food could grow,
shared the pot to fatten everyone,
read pages, taught a generation to write
and speak for themselves.
I'm just following routine now,
until I hear inside me say:
I'm done."

We hum, searching memories,
tracing back time to a house at Cowper Street
where folktales, songs and board-games
tied love not then fully understood.
He laughs, remembers the words to
Bob Marley's "Three Little Birds",
Don't worry about a thing
every little thing is gonna be alright.
And I knew then, every little thing
would be alright.

EVERYBODY BUSINESS BUT DEM OWN

God forbid if di chatty mouth ooman
ever ketch up in your business.
Laawd help you
if she ever hear one cross word or bad,
never mind di whole story.
She noh need it,
she's too busy flying pan auto-pilot,
tu'n inventor by text message and phonecall.
She'll add her own bits and bats
to fill the gaps in the story,
create a whole soap opera.
She loves to hear the latest,
hottest, talking headlines
straight out of the community –
who's died, their ailments,
the cause of death,
whose marriage is up in problems,
who stole government benefits
to buy a show-off fancy car,
who's pregnant again,
who's the baby father,
who's gaarn pan holiday
when they don't have a job,
who's walking the streets with dem shoes-front buss.

She's chatty, chatty, labba, labba –
mercy me, she noh easy!
She ah labrish,
spread the tale like butter:
I can't believe its not butter – it's true!
She's up to speed with the whole affair
of yesterday's and today's news,
tomorrow's predictions at the ready.

Flapping in the spirit of chit chat,
she can't kibba her mouth.
And what ah tribulation
if she ever come to your house –
she can tell wha' gwan with your family,
your shopping list, what's in your fridge.
And if you offer her tea,
watch her, watch her good,
but not for too long
because she nar form nah fool.
When argument buss out,
she will teck foot and gaarn
only to chat every detail of your behaviour
to someone else,
how you show up yourself,
airing your dirty laundry,
how yu dress like puss and wear old slippers.

She's mastered the art form,
crafted her style,
but she nar get no prize fi her deeds
cos she too inna, inna,
damn blasted fas' and cantankerous!

HONESTY AND FORGIVENESS

It was the Church of the Holy Faithful annual summer convention. A visiting pastor from Sheffield come to deliver the sermon on Honesty and Forgiveness. With visitors from all over, it was also a convention of ladies' church hats.

400 people fill the old wooden benches; another 90 or so stand in the wings. The Holy Faithful choir sings, "What a friend we have in Jesus", as Pastor Charles leans forward onto di pulpit and opens his bible.

Sister Dean, di usher from the Church, was in charge of greeting and seating Pastor wife, Sister Charles, and other distinguish guest. Now Sister Dean tek she role very serious, as serious as the word of the Lord, and her hats! That day, she wore a deep rose-pink hat with two large ostrich feathers and a big bow hitched up on di side. As she ushered the guest, di congregation couldn't help but feast dey eyes on it. "What a hat, ee…!" "Dat's a winning hat!" some exclaim. Others muttered, "It's too big and showy for church and she just ah tek di shine away from di matter of di convention."

Sister Dean, she never really business with what people have to say, all she wants is for her hat to shine up to di Lord. She sit up front with Pastor wife, and beside Sister James, who from the time she see di big bow and di pink feathers ah sway and ah bounce, she start to roll her eyes and fix her hat.

Once the choir finish singing, Pastor didn't waste anytime, him gone deep into him sermon. Pulling back his breath, he seh, "Open your hearts and let the spirit of the Lord overtake you and cleanse you of your sins… Love the wrongdoer and the backbiter and bring them to the way of the Lord. Tell them thy Lord loves them; share the good news of our Father who died for us… Forgive them, like our Father forgives his children! … I don't think you hear me! I said! Forgive them like our Father forgives his children… Can I get a witness?" The choir sings out 'Amen' as pastor voice deh ah whoop, his words suspend in mid air!

"Praaaise the Lord. Yes Jeeesus!" The congregation repeats, "Preach Pastor, preach." Pastor seh "Can I get a witness…"

Sister Dean jump up from her seat, stands before Pastor, spins and talks in tongues. "Yes Jesus! Ah hamna hummna hamna, praise the Lord! Preach, Pastor preach!" Pastor seh, "The lamb of God." Bandsmen start strum guitar along with piano and di drummer. Sister Dean fling her hands up, and next ting her hat fly off, straight into Sister James' lap, where Pastor wife catch sight of Sister James ah examine it.

At di end of di service, Sister Dean, coming out of di spirit, tries to fix herself, while congratulating Pastor Charles at di same time, but before she could find her second breath to put two words together, Sister James steps right in front and greets Pastor and his wife, "What a righteous service, Pastor. You said all the right things. And, Sister Dean, what a way the spirit touch you. You nearly lose your new hat."

A smiling young lady comes to thank Sister Dean for inviting her to church, and tell her she look lovely in the hat she sold her. "You would never know it was second hand." Sister James curl her lip tight and seh, "Oooh, I don't like old things." Pastor wife seh, "But you like that one." Well, if you ever see how dog tun vex wid puss! Sister James tun fi er head sideways and squint fi er eye like when wind ah blow, seh "Puppa Jesus, if any body hear mi dying trial, it's not a sin to like a hat, Sister Charles. Is shame you want put in mi eye, especially after Pastor sermon? Furthermore, member seh, dere's nuttin like ah shame ole lady… Dem sey when Pastor gone home to Jamaica to bury him mother, it was twelve months before him come back, an yuh with child."

Mouth drop and ear prick up, for who cudda more honest in dem chatting than Sister James? Pastor wife, she couldn't do anymore other than find di forgiveness, for her husband di tan up right there… She straighten her back and seh, "Sister James, you didn't hear what Pastor said? 'Love the wrong doer and the backbiter and bring them to the lord!' Now can I get a witness and an 'amen', and di name of di shop where Sister Dean bought her hat!"

INNA DE DANCEHALL

By the 1990s, the roots & culture sound systems and back to Afrika movement seemed to fade in the voices of the dancehall DJ's. Raggamuffin gold teeth, slackness talk and ghetto fabulous became the anthem, and lyrical Gun Don and Mr Lover Man clashed for the title of Don Gorgon, & Donnette fought all comers for the title of Dancehall Queen.

RAMDANCE MASTER

Dancehall
deejay
ramdance
master
wid yuh crew-cut fade,
etched dollar sign, razor sharp
S-curls and waves under de du-rag,
a true,
a you
set di trend
and di standard,
a true
a you
de people dem prefer.

Set for
water pumpy,
freedom floods dance floors
so hot, so pepper,
so cool and deadly,
in de heat of the night,
sleng teng dancing
till a dawn.

De Selecta spins vinyl,
fresh studio cuts crackle smooth,
riddim ease through the bass,
gathering sing-jays, deejays
lyrical Dons
toasting in season
over de tune.
Nuff man and woman
jus' a heng on.

Dem jus' a sway
and a ride de riddim.

Gyal dem hold tight to boasty mouth
of Shabba Ranks' *World of Girls*,
Tingalingaling, school bell ring;
Dis yah lover man is praised
in de current of hand waves.

Words clash at de microphone stand
as Tiger Man, Cutty Ranks,
Ninja Man recite odes,
and de twenty-one gun-talk
of Dons cuffing Sound boys
triggers sound salute.
Dons big bout yah in de sea of de night ravers
bawl forward to reeewind
Haul and pull it, Selecta,
and come back again.

Dancehall Deejay,
ramdance master,
wid yuh crew-cut and fade,
dollar marking pencilled
razor sharp, and slick and click suit,
Travel Fox yu wear.
A true, a you, a you, a you, a you
de people dem prefer.

DANCEHALL SOUND CLASH

I reminisce on heartical times
when Sir Coxsone did rub-a-dub
with cool vibes, an' Saxon
toast bonafide bionic rhymes.

I reminisce dancehall 1980's style,
with an exodus of speaker boxes
in old vans ready to line walls
at Chapeltown Community Centre,

where wires spiral through soundman hands,
connect dread man at de control tower
with turntable, amplifier and tweeter,
selected sounds of Mama Africa's sons:

Marley, Tosh, D Brown, Jacob Miller,
Jamrock raw roots reggae riddims:
Do you know what it means to have a revolution?
And what it takes to make a solution
Fighting against oppression,
Battering down depression?

In the height of sound clash
Manchester and Leeds strike a match.
Baron high power came to test tunes,
Fugitive sound boys head dem swell,
along with Sparta, Maverick,
Emperor, Genesis and Channel One.

In London, King Tubby came too,
dropped dub plates inna de dance.
But Jungle Warrior crew got fresh
with a deeper cylinder-charge in the bass-line.

Revolutionary sounds of Rasta
weaved through headwraps,
beaver hats, red, gold and green tams,
and dreams of the promised land.

Irie skanking, lean-foot youths
in Clarks' heels and Bally brand boots,
Sistrens in pencil-pleated skirts,
armed with passion eena rub a dub dance,

lick wood, praise Jah, summon
order to Selecta fe *Lift it up*,
pull it back, an come again.
In dis, I and I reminisce.

GRANGE AVENUE

It only took half a sun to silhouette
and cut di sky to draw a crowd of people
to the streets. You wud tink seh
one somebody come back from the West Indies
all shine teet an' give wey mango for free.

If yu ever sight sound boys ah balance an' a move sound box,
dat heavy load of craftsmanship stack to shake
the concrete, and resurrect houses to harmonies
of roots reggae sounds;
watch dem string up and wire up,
see di DJ procession line up pon di testing, testing,
pon di microphone, check, check,
before di selector runs riddim,
unleash ah music selection
from inside him box to drop pon di deck.

Inna di Granges, dis was strictly roots to di culture.
Wait deh! Ah who deh a toast, draw breath
pon di mic control? Ah KD Ranko
Nuff people chat behind my back…
champion a champion, bantan a bantan,
an di one Stylo. Who deh singjay?
Clifford Irie, Sweet Voice, Frank
from Nyah Tribesman an di one Fluid Irie.
Man seh turn up di mix, mix me down,
fire up di echo chamber,
play di dub plate done drop at dance clash
di toppa notch tune fi draw back.

Whether ah speaker box carrier or di operator,
or ah DJ toaster, di sound engineer,
selector or cali herbsman,

here natty roots people twist back bottle cap,
sip malt, ginseng or a cold Lucozade.

From frontline Hayfield Pub, Cantor's,
di Gambling House and Darkie's blues,
nuff tan tuddy, some just ah satah
'til di avenue and corner cork,
in di niceness of di vibes
people just ah rock to di tunes…

DANCEHALL QUEEN

(Man a don, woman a donnette)

Donnette, dancehall queen,
butterfly's knock-kneeing style
and pattern, her fashion de latest
outa New York, Paris and London,
the originator of Jamdown ghetto fabulous,
royalty hot-footing dancehall arenas,
flexing blue, pink, green,
and yellow peacock hair weaves,
gold teeth, diamond crepe,
Miss Wire Waist, mampi batty riding,
glamour at its best,
Dj's crown her Dancehall Queen,
Donnette reigns supreme,
for she naar jest.

JAZZ FUNK
(for Dovell Morton)

The testament is jazz funk,
rhythm pressed onto 12-inch
vinyl records; the DJ plays backbeats,
synthesized whispers of horns and
strings so electrifying dancers resonate
beyond the sweep of feet.
On the tip of brassy notes,
bodies turn to sweat on
the dance floor.

As a trumpet screams African-soul,
jazz-funkin' for Jamaica,
on Herbie Hancock's
black n white ivory keys,
out of many soul-head dancers flows
a fist of power, a brotha
polished in the groove.
With James Brown's jazz magic
in his feet, he elevates from the mix,
the lightning waves of sound,
a spiritual transformation
tuned like a train, a train coming.
When he gets on board the groove,
the devil can't touch this bass extension,
a revolution in motion,
a warrior charge,
a jazz funk Congo drum dance.

In the battle for the heaviest
on the club dance floor, he was born,
but time, time moved on,
in the hardcore beat of funk
in the jazz of it.

In the depression of a jobless
society, he had more
to express in his feet, the sprats and
pants he wore,
to be the greatest.
Like Muhammad Ali he was
a breath of hope, to say it loud,
dance it proud,
but like the jazz funk era he died
with the music and was buried with
stories of back in the days
when jazz-funk ruled the airwaves.

PUNK ROCK RIVER

Toffee-nosed folk better retreat,
there's anarchy in the voices
of the young ones, tangled
in their fathers' boot laces,
spit 'n polish docs, red white and blue flags,
lacquer and spiked hair, beer cans and cheap cider.
No one's got a job,
no future to think about,
so who gives a damn it's the Royal Jubilee?
God save the queen, sing the Pistols,
wear a crown stitched with pins
and the jubilee mug for the mantel's
soon chipped, got no handles.
In a winter of discontent and the Iron lady,
there's lots of reasons to kick down
the Berlin wall, shock em,
pogo dance to the sounds of punk rock bass,
scream chaos, and never mind the bollocks.

THIS IS LOVERS ROCK

At 3 am, the dip so and rock so
of this music begins,
a reflection of a not-so-easy life,
a Black British fusion
of new soul-reggae sounds.
We come alive, dancing like butter
melting on the skins of Lovers Rock,
rubbing away sorrows
as words of love are reborn
in the heat of bodies rubbing
thigh to thigh, waistlines held tight,
rebel natty in Farah and Gabicci,
holding tight Long Life and Colt 45;
sisters in chiffon and crepe-pleated dresses,
drinks of babycham, snowballs,
bacardi and coke clutched
behind their natties' backs;
all flexing till morning,
till blood boils to heaven's gates.
Dancers stew like peas, split the seams
of the paper on front room walls.

Louisa Mark's 'Sixth Street' plays;
in the lyrical tide of high notes
comfort is found; Janet Kay's
Silly Games is on the deck.
Ravers call for pull up and rewind
to catch back a dance.

I've been wanting you,
for so long it's a shame, oh baby,
every time I hear your name,
oh the pain...

The settlement is in the words;
without effort the wanting
to be loved never changes.
Dance don't cease here.
Pick your style, bubblers of the night,
no fuss, no fight
everything just nice.

GET UP STAND UP
(*MC Revolution*)

Get up, stand up!
There's a revolution.
The youth dem
ah 16-bar MC,
free-style lyrical architect chanters,
Dre beats wired through phones.
Dem ah jam tune
on street corners,
dem ah waddle and ah bounce
in ah cipher,
saggy-styled G-star,
Nike Kicks philosophers.

Shhh… listen to the ancient griot heartbeat,
chattin' the woes of this generation,
a thousand unanswered questions
rhymed into stanzas,
rippin' pon de microphone
spittin' in ah style
to bass-lines in banter.
See dem assume a rude boy stance
with the same slang in dem wordsmith mouth:
Jah knows! Wha gwaan! Blood! Easy my yout!

Rhythms still flow like water
to tell you their dreams.
The DJ's, presidents
of scratch 'n mix tape samplers,
manz dem hold tight into da laters,
into de early hours.

But do they know where the hard core
bass-line riddims come from,
know the de hard time stylee,
where cold ground was my bed last night
and rock was my pillow too?

Does David Oluwale, Olive Morris,
the Mangrove 9 and the New Cross Fire,
ring any bells today?
Does *Jah knows Blood* mean the
same as God knows everything?

I hear de yout man chatting
and I wonder about dem struggle,
the absent fathers and mothers who have
less time to keep things ship-shape.
Does dem granny cooking
still sweet dem, and is her Dutch pot of stories
more than just the name of the local takeaway?

Their beauty still shines, eyes swell regular
at the grave side – another death in the zone,
postcodes where if you reach twenty-one it's a blessing.

I wonder why I'm asking all
these questions; am I just
getting old?

THE CROWNING

Empress, dread queens, kings,
children of the African diaspora,
come draw your circle of listeners.

Speak your truth on legacy of empire,
enslaved-packed ships where ancestors
were tossed like pebbles into the ocean.

Come warriors, soul rebels,
singers of the blues, spirits of the purple dawn,
bring us Solomon's wiser history,

for we are readers, pen-stressors,
dust blowers from basement libraries,
knowledge stackers and frequent travellers.

In the natural mystic breeze, we de lion,
in the whirlwind we de flag –
the red black green of it.

In Garvey's starliner
we connect the mediums
beyond the ships.

Bring your melodies, song-makers,
chants and dance; reclaim we name
and bury the pain.

Bring to the ceremonies clay pots,
calabashes, incense and oils,
tell de people dem fe come,

come with your head wraps
and ginny heads, come with your cornrows,
Afros and your natty dreads.

Bring harmony and comeliness
and the wisdom in your navel string;
bring the ancient prescriptions,

bring priests, drums, silk-white robes,
burn seven oils in seven corners for seven days,
read nine psalms of David without ceasing.

Come purify we so we recognise
the Conquering Lion
of the tribe of Judah

Jah Ras Tafari
Jah Ras Tafari
Jah Ras Tafari

LOG-BOOK

DAYS UNFOLD A NEW BEGINNING

…birds wishing to share the fruits of love…

Days unfold a new beginning
in a season of migration,
two birds fan wings in unison
make sweet liquid sounds in the sky,
seductively steal each other's hearts.
Radiant as a peacock's tail,
longing to fly, she flaps passionately
to see if greener grass grows across the pond.
He nestles in the windy city
between soft poetic notes,
smoky skyscrapers,
highways, trains and bridges.

Two birds of fantasy sing
day and night to rearrange
the direction of the crescent moon
in favour of tropical desires.
Love's stream narrows
into a whirlpool; rain brews;
a senseless cold breeze blows,
arouses hot and fiery argument,
melts wings in peppery winds.

In a crazy flight of fancy
two birds wheel and turn.
Now they flutter through photo galleries
asking with whom lies the fault,
only to seek a different beginning,
a new beginning, the bittersweet
taste of love.

1983

It was winter in the city of white roses,
and first rain, then sun, shone like
a milky rainbow blend of molasses.
A reggae-smooth sound boy
as soft as fudge brown,
bold with street-soul moves,
funky club grooves,
came to cultivate love,
water affection with whispers
over candlelit dinners for two –
readymade cheese coleslaw
canned pilchards with oil slick.
He tied his sisters' silk ribbons
into neat bows on used gifts,
rapped words on riddims tracks.
Our waist and thighs
arched against wall, we danced,
rubbed off wallpaper into damp scrolls;
a 1000 volts of John Holts' velvet-soft voice
says the right words
he can't express.
Discovering puppy love we melted
like plastic to Luther Vandross,
always and forever
until the sun was eclipsed.

1989

Into the core of the Big Apple
like a fantasy he came, real fine,
a figure of the moon's lips'
black harmony, the touch of essence.
He was sandalwood, ink scrawls and water-
cushions, fairy tales and Guyanese kisses.
Duration. One year.
Love, *always and forever*.

2000

Permission to ride an emotion,
untie faith, sing the blues –
once bitten and better must come –
dat's an old time song that
hangs like strange fruit in a northern wind.
Take your pick
mind you don't pick *sh*t* –
the kind that look sweet.

2003

In the heat
of summer madness,
we shared our favourite books,
laughed as if we knew each other
from way back in the days,
exchanged glances as if the mountain
was the peak.

You look like Lauryn Hill with yah thick dreadlocks in yah hat.
Funny, I always thought she looked like me!

In the midst of Bath's breeze
the night revealed secrets,
the last page of blues renditions.
Endless is your heart.

ANOTHER CROSSING

Water no get enemy
— Femi Kuti

BIRD OF AFRICA

Here I come again,
like a bennu riding on the wind,
crossing oceans to dock on river banks
between the mangroves.

Here I come, five hundred years
of pinioned wings stretching
into the Gambian sea
of *barakas, djembi* drum calls;
into the hot, wet air I fly.

Here I sweat away
a stolen past, slake a throat
parched from dusty red roads,
alighting to hot tin roofs, thatched mud huts
and sweltering nights,
servings of bread (and the strange look
of bush meat), retreating from the rain of white flies
while the river embraces the sunset melodies
of Garnett Silk, *Hello Mama Africa, how are you?*
Play, pause, press rewind three times.
Watch the moonlit water flicker,
scratch away the pain of mosquitoes
welcoming me home.

It feels like yesterday,
pulling back the curtain of the past
to hear the griot singing for the healing
of five hundred broken years,
twenty million or more stolen voices
from the motherland.

WESTMORELAND

A bird's eye view over Westmoreland Parish
plays like a roots reggae tune, retuned like
saffron winds across green hills, red rich soil;
I sing of country living, where winding roads lead
to Springfield hills, to sit with fireflies
and the mosquitoes' hum in the evening breeze.
Under cali heat and orange skies the air changes;
here, nature's breath rekindles kindness,
mangoes, lime and coconut trees,
and I suck the sweet jelly and sap of cane,
juice running down my hand.
I recall my mother talking of single-bible nectar
so I cut it to wash Afro locks in the spring,
drink it to wash out the hurt
of love's pulse gone to earth.
Between the rocks and stones
silence sits under the trees;
the current doesn't rush
to tatter thoughts teased by fresh spring water,
though not far away the roaring river flows.
As the Ciboney once were, I am
in the settlement of my mind
on the cliff sides and hills of Westmoreland.
Healed, the whispers of salt
draw me to the seashore,
where silky sand shines smooth against my skin,
the mood of the sun resurrects the melanin tint
and black brown bronze bodies on the beach
look like boats out at sea.

FRENCHMAN'S BAY

'There is no greater invitation to love than loving first'
– St. Augustine of Hippo

The dawn smiled while tenderness
was patient with sun-fresh eyes

over the rocks of Frenchman's Bay
where gold in black sand glistened

like fertile jewels against skin;
trees slow-danced gently

to the sound of the sea calling
to baptise desire;

gracefully, the cool of the breeze
hugged the contours of the waves;

agreeably full and thin bodies
palm-twist themselves into curls of locks;

sweetness of fresh coconut water
quenched the communion of desire;

Roots son of the island enticed
the first moment of new breath.

Memory returns time after time,
Mavado's song "I'm on the Rock"

flows into the shadow cast by moonlight,
dreams birthed by love drift apart.

LONG-TIME NO SEE
A VISIT TO MY AUNTY BLOSSOM IN SPANISH TOWN

Lard! Look pon mi sister daughter
long-time no see.
Your mudda call mi from Inglan',
said you're at your uncle Pop's house.
Mi know you couldn't come a Jamaica
and don't come see mi in Spanish Town
But wait…?
You really resemble your mudda,
your Daddy Mac's granddaughter for true;
that's a McLaren smile.
I see your Grandmother Eugenie –
what a way yuh fingers dem tall.
Do you sew? Mi mudda use to sew, make pretty
bed linen to sell in the market,
gather ole crocus bags; you mudda
spend di whole day a bang out di flour
pon rock stone, until she favour ghost.
There was a lot of us in di family,
eight from mi mudda and father –
mi sister Violet, her father different.
Mi father was a handsome man, not too tall;
he was high up in the Lodge, a member of all kind of tings,
travelling the island. One ting, him love him white rum.
Dem gone now, buried with memories.
Two sister and two brother settle a foreign
to make dem way in life. Not me,
I never want to leave Jamaica.
Not me, mi born here, mi fine here,
follow my mudda footsteps
in trading before my knees turn bad,
travelled to Panama, Cuba and America,
but dem days gone, mi get ole.
Which month you born?

"August."
Mi know a something make mi just come to love you;
you share di same month as me.
Over forty years since you mudda gone a Inglan',
she leave one son born here –
him no stop going on wid him ways,
but you mudda always call.
Inglan' never tek mi fancy.
I went to America, but I never like it.
Mi love Jamaica and mi know you could never
come to Jamaica and don't come to Spanish Town
to see mi. Laard, what a way you favour we bad!

ROOTZ RUNNIN I

Up deh, inna Lawrence Tavern,
Right up deh where di sugar cane grows,
deh mi great grandad daddy
sweat could've watered di soil.
Imagine him: steadfast, bent and buckled;
wid ah machete sharp and swift
him cut and release di sugary liquid
that make di rum we now offer in remembrance
of di McLaren name in the family line.
But ask I myself, Who is McLaren?
Could he be di one dat did own all dese acres,
before we knew we deh free
to drink dis rum as sweet as blood
an sunshine, as we pour it to the soil
and remember who we deh call on
to know we not stronger than we roots?

ROOTS RUNNIN II

Up deh! Right up deh in Lawrence Tavern,
amongst di tree an bush where she rest in peace,
Great Grandmother Tamar McLaren
planted plenty good seeds,
planted mango and breadfruit trees,
yam and cassava, dis ole time Jamaica oomen
chopped back and forth tobacco leaves,
pulled on smoke-filled clay pipe
with the lighted bowl in her mouth,
cooked pots of provision inna di ground,
embroidered traditions of alchemy,
grated bissy 'n ginger an white rum
to run di pain out from bad-belly,
bruk disease an fever to strengthen
these branches for another crossing,
three generations kindling life
right here in the city of Leeds.

RETURNING HOME – ANOTHER CROSSING
(For Travis Johnson OBE)

Yuh cum a Inglan suh long, long ago,
from de island of wood and springs,
Blue Mountains so high, sun so hot,
three counties and fourteen parishes.

With a twinkle in yuh eyes, a twirl
of yuh hat, yuh left your family ties
way, way back in 1962.
Everything you knew about life

was where yuh come from;
a young, daring, strong-boned
eighteen-years-old, yuh come clear
cross de ocean with yuh sweet talk

an' luggage in yuh hand, yuh suitcase filled
with what yuh own, what yuh could carry,
with ambition to achieve and de promise
to return home some day.

Over forty year and more, yuh deh a
Inglan in the cold, with its
fenky sunshine and plenty rain fall;
yuh drive bus and train for British Rail,

and still nothing match yuh smile like
yuh wife Betsy and yuh children
and yuh love for back home,
where yuh dream to build a house.

You was man of many words, set
yuh mind to management structure
of Leeds Jamaican society.
With ideas of unity and social rights

yuh brought people from all over,
Jamaica High Commissioner,
dignitaries too much to mention –
even poet and folklorist Miss Lou pass through,

originate her ideas of a Jamaica House
where people coulda gather and stay.
A storyteller, campaigner, race
relation adviser, housing matters,

and churchgoer: yuh knew it all.
Yuh set a plan with yuh wife to go
back home, put down money to buy
bricks and mortar to build yuh house

and make better yuh dream of home,
fit for a king and his queen.
When time came, yuh pack yuh days up
inna Inglan, your jobs well done.

Mi never tink I would reach Jamaica
and hear yuh name call, how yuh house
so pretty, till eyes tun red.
Dear Mr Johnson, yuh never live

long enough to enjoy de dream,
but yuh knew something more
than we, since yuh gone pon another
crossing to a bigger and better place.

WE BURY OUR DEAD

My mother's hands
bound family ties
near and far,
pick up
a long distance call
to bury our dead.

Jamaica cries,
Kingston's sadness sweats tears:
six gun shots to the head,
a grandson dead.

Dusted hats and polished shoes in procession
at Dovecot cemetery;
I gaze at satin, grey-beaded mules
stained to burnt orange,
dust licking crevices under the soles of feet.
Preacher man says:
We must love our brother.
The Lord God is our saviour.
The choir sings over the coffin.
Loved ones swell tears into red dirt.
We bury our dead.

Watery smiles from kinsfolk
and friends with tales of what used to be
and better must come.
Rum offerings pour from hands to honour the departed,
and dancing tongues bring duppy stories,
lash white rum.
We bury our dead.

Kingston's heat at Dovecot cemetery.
A polished procession:

preacher man, choir, loved ones and bronze, shining coffin.
Into red dirt we tears swell,
wet eyes guide heaven's gates.
We pray, we bury our dead.

At the corner of life
my mother's arms bring us together.
I hear Jamaica cry, long distance call,
to bury our dead.

WHEN MY TIME COME

"The lord is my shepherd I shall not want,
He maketh me to lie down in green pastures"
— Psalm 23

Mi dear chile,
we are livin' in our last days,
so when mi time come,
I waant to be buried in mi red suit,
the one I just buy.

I buy a new one every five years
just for de occasion,
I like to keep with the fashion
and dis suit favour de roses in my garden —
you know how I love dem so.

So look here, child,
when mi time come I waant you
to remember
dis is de suit I waant to be buried in,
de red one right here,
trailing from neck to hem
wid beads and silk embroidery
just like royalty,
a colour of importance.
I saw de queen wearing one just like it pon TV.

So remember wat mi show you;
see how it tailor stitched in and out
with good threads,
like mi granny use to do.
She bury in red too.

And when de Lord calls
I want to be wearing a red suit,
de one I handpick especially –
I walk de whole day till carn bun mi toes.

I like to look good at all times,
no-one is going to say
I never dress away till de end of my days.
Mi buy mi suit from Marks and Spencer,
all mi underwear too,
put dem in de trunk
with all mi fine nightwear and tings,
fold in camphor balls.
Mi a ole woman, 75 years just gone,
but mi a no fool,
mi make all mi plans;
put down insurance
fe horse-drawn carriage,
gospel singers, saxophone player,
and a red rose for each and every one.

Mi no waant bury a England,
mi waant mi ashes spread cross de River
Thames, make de waves teck
mi back to which part mi did come from.

And when all and sundries come to the house,
start dig, stake claim to what dem waant,
to wat dem no waant,
when tears flare and tongues clash difference,
I want my daughter to remember
dis is the red suit I waant to be buried in,

the red one, right here.

KINDRED

Curly Locks,
your mudda is an African,
cut from a navel cord of life songs,
rain of yesterdays, red, gold and green
living melodies, silver 'n cowries,
pulse of Maroon, Fante
or Yoruba blood packed tight
from middle passage, a heartbeat of stories.

Girl child, you came in the middle of de night
when all were asleep.
A sage woman spoke to cleanse;
Oshun and moon drummed verses.

True, you favour your mudda eena da eyes,
but you have your daddy's kinks and locks
and his round cherry-blossom smile.
God Merciful and Kind,
You name Rhiema, a princess soon to be queen of these truths.

Your grandfather's mother, Great Granny Lucilda came
with home-blends of coconut oil,
Nanna Gloria with green Dax to wax your plaits
and stories of Great Granny Eugenie –
a higgler woman who stood no taller than five feet –
and I, with oils, sandalwood and cocoa butter,
come down de line to anoint your crown
so your dreads drink oils made
since the time of Eve and our beginnings.

NOTES AND REFERENCES

p. 12.

Where is the Love – Black Eyed Peas, from *Elephunk.*

Garvey – Marcus Garvey (1887-1940), Jamaican who became the leader of the United Negro Improvement Association and advocate of Back to Africa.

Kinky Reggae – Bob Marley, from *Catch a Fire* (1973)

p. 13.

idren – Rastafarian version of bredrin (brother).

The Brotherhood – was a Leeds-based group of African Caribbean activists of the 1970s. From it grew the *Uhuru* movement (qv). Despite its name, the Brotherhood involved women.

We'll be for ever loving Jah – Bob Marley, from the *Uprising* album (1980)

p. 19.

jacks and hot rice – children's games. Jacks (aka knucklebones or dibs, was played with small six-pointed plastic or metal objects and a bouncy ball. Hot rice was a game that involved the child who was *on* or *it,* avoiding being hit by the ball thrown by other players.

Dem favour leggo beast – they are behaving like wild animals!

p. 20.

(Say it loud) I'm Black and I'm Proud – James Brown, from a two-part single released in 1968.

Steel Pulse – great Black British roots reggae band from Handsworth Birmingham. Their early albums included *Handsworth Revolution* (1978) and *Tribute to the Martyrs* (1979)

Ras Daniel Heartman – (1942-1990), a Rastafarian Jamaican artist whose iconic print of a dreadlocked child graced many walls.

Harriet Tubman – (c 1822-1913), African American abolitionist and suffragist, famous for her part in organising the "underground railway" of safe houses for escaping enslaved people.

p. 21.

River bank Coverly – a Jamaican folk song.

Paul Bogle (c. 1820-1865) – the Baptist minister who led a peasants' revolt against colonial oppression in Jamaica from at Morant Bay in 1865, who, along with hundreds of African Jamaicans was executed by the British in a savage act of revenge.

p. 22.

We speak to you by parables – words from the Rosicrucian manifesto, which continues: "We speak unto you by parables, but would willingly bring you to the right, simple, easy, and ingenuous exposition, understanding, declaration, and knowledge of all secrets." Rosicrucianism has its roots in alchemical and hermetic philosophy dating from the sixteenth century. In the twentieth century it had followers of esoteric Christianity, connections with masonry and the Golden Dawn (of which W.B. Yeats was a member). Rosicrucianism spread to the Caribbean, probably in the late 19th century, where there are still lodges in most islands.

p. 25.

Unoo favour heng pon nail – unkempt, raggedy, i.e. like clothes which have been hanging on a nail.

p. 26.

Love Thy Neighbour – a popular and controversial British sitcom (1972-1976) featuring black and white couples – controversial because of the explicit racism of the white husband, but often popular with the Caribbean community because the black couple stood up for themselves.

Black and White Minstrels – a popular, long-running light entertainment show (1958-1978) in black face, shameful for its racism. It took the BBC eleven years to take it off air, following protests against it beginning in 1967.

Jim Davidson's Chalky – a crude, racist caricature from the late 1970s of a West Indian 'Chalky White' whose opening line was "Day-light come and I gotta sign on".

Lynch's Spanish Tina reproduction – J.H. Lynch (1911-1989) whose kitch, gently erotic print of the sultry Tina (the print hints at her nakedness) just managed to stay on the right side of respectability. Hugely popular in the 1970s and early 80s.

Blue Spot radiogram – Barcelona Blaupunkt – top of the range in rosewood and popular with the Caribbean community in the 1950s and 1960s.

dub versions – the multiple uses that could be made of a single track in the production of Jamaican reggae 45s, including instrumentals with the singer's track floating in and out, with plenty of bass and reverb (King Tubby was the star) and spoken, chanted tracks by dj's such as *U Roy* (*Version Galore*) and *Big Youth* (*Screaming Target*).

Desmond Dekker ('Israelites') *Jimmy Cliff* ('Many Rivers to Cross') and *Millie Small* ('My Boy Lollipop') were the ska to reggae singers who first broke into the British pop charts.

pickney – child

p. 27.

A blues, rub-a-dub – Blues parties or shabeens were held in the basements of private homes in the days when there were few public spaces for West

Indians in Britain. Perhaps because space was limited, *rub-a-dub*, dancing up very close, grinding the hips together, was the favoured style. The babycham box was used to dim the lights.

mannish water – goat's head soup – reputed to assist men's "performance"!

fass – as in fast, a forward, precocious child.

Sir Yankee record shop – was a converted garage at the back of Gathorne Terrace and Spencer Place (Leeds), the first place to sell imported Jamaican records.

Cimarons – one of the first British reggae groups, formed 1967. Their first album was *In Time* (1974).

Electric Press – originally a factory on Great George Street (Leeds) that housed a carriage-making works and a printing works. Part of the building became a venue for performance in the 1980s, with a stage. It now houses the Carriage Works theatre and several restaurants and bars.

Bunny Wailer – one of the original Wailers with Bob Marley and maker of one of the very best reggae albums of all time – *Blackheart Man* (1976).

Green Shield stamps – from the 1950s up until 1991, when they were withdrawn, shoppers kept books to paste these trading stamps in, which could then be exchanged for goods.

black jack and Bazooka Joes – respectively a liquorishy toffee and bubblegum that could be bought for a penny.

p. 29.

Harehills Middle – the 9-13 school no longer exists, but in its time it was distinguished as the place where Phoenix Dance was born, under the guidance of Nadine Senior. See http://mcnultymedia.co.uk/blog/2013/03/reflections-on-the-dance-phenomenon-at-harehills-middle-school/

the bump – a 70's dance – bumping hips.

Dainty toffees – a penny "chew".

Spanish – the Leeds/Yorkshire term for liquorice (but known elsewhere in the UK).

Savoury vinegar crisps – briefly made by Smiths in the 1980s? and very popular at 4, Gathorne Mount.

Bush player – a stereogram from the 1970s.

p. 31.

Paradise Lost – was the name of the dance featured on the *In the City* television programme made about Harehills in 1979. See http://mcnultymedia.co.uk/i2m2/clients/broadcast/chapeltown/yorkshire_evening_post_2.php

p. 32.

hard-dough – or hardo bread, a Jamaican bread.

Roots – a TV series based on Alex Haley's 1976 novel of that name. It was

99

broadcast in the UK in 1977. Kunte Kinte and Kizzy were both characters from the series.

NF – National Front, far right, white racist organisation founded in 1967, precursor to the British Movement in infamy.

p. 33.

Clarks shoes – an iconic item of dress for young West Indians, celebrated in reggae and dancehall, both in the Caribbean and in the UK. There is even a book about Clarks, Al Fingers, *Clarks in Jamaica*.

No 72 – was the house of the Rastarian Twelve Tribes on Harehills Avenue, Leeds.

niyabinghi drums – the three drums of the Rastarian "grounation" or meeting. Listen to any Count Ossie recording.

natty – dreadlocks or an Afro turning into dreadlocks.

p. 35.

Rivers of Blood – Enoch Powell's infamous racist speech of 1968.

One Down, a Million to Go – a National Front chant.

No Blacks, No Dogs, No Irish – a landlord's sign photographed in London in 1966.

p. 37.

Maureen Baker – who died in 2012, was a radical community activist, originally from Ireland, who fought for the rights of black people and travellers and was an anti-apartheid campaigner.

Mrs Paul – Mrs Gertrude Paul was appointed the first black headteacher in Leeds, at the former Elmhurst Middle School in 1976. As part of the United Caribbean Association she was responsible for organising a team of black lawyers, led by Rudy Narayan, from London to defend the youths arrested in the bonfire night riot. Those youths whom this team defended were acquitted. The campaign against the arrests and trial linked *Chapeltown News* and the London-based monthy *Race Today* magazine, run by the Race Today Collective led by activists such as Darcus Howe, Farrukh Dhondy and Linton Kwesi Johnson.

p. 38.

sus laws – the police right to stop and question in the street "on suspicion", whose misuse against black youth provoked many of the early 1980s black uprisings.

UB40 – the number on the signing-on document to claim unemployment benefit.

the dole – unemployment benefit.

p. 39.

poll-tax – Margaret Thatcher's hugely unpopular attempt to switch the cost of property rates onto individuals, penalising poorer families; it was abandoned after poll-tax riots.

Maggie snatched milk – as Minister for Education who cut free school milk to the over 7s. The cry was "Maggie Thatcher, Milk Snatcher".

like a zebra crossing – the reported words of Neville Staple of the Specials at the Rock Against Racism concert in Potternewton Park, Leeds.

p. 40.

did the wop – a 1980s dance associated with hip-hop that mostly involved moving the upper body.

The Wag – a club on Wardour Street London of the 1980s, with a diverse crowd and range of music, black and white, with a space for reggae.

Talkin' Blues – Bob Marley, original 1973 recording, released on album of the same name in 1991.

Genesis FM – a Leeds pirate radio station which went on air in 1992.

p. 41.

Back to Life – Soul to Soul, in which Caron Wheeler was featured singer.

There's nothing like this – Omar (Lye-Fook) reached the charts with this in 1991.

p. 42.

Churchill – in 1939, Winston Churchill, talking to West Indian sugar producers, said: "Our possessions of the West Indies, like that of India, gave us strength... to lay the foundation of... our great position in the world."

In treating man... – from *The Poetical Works of Marcus Garvey*, p. 37.

p. 44.

Dutch pot – or dutchie, a heavy cast-iron pot used in Jamaica, originally with three feet so a fire could be lit underneath.

labba labba – Jamaican patois, to gossip, to chat indiscreetly.

higgler – usually a market woman or street seller.

p. 45.

Ken Boothe – (1948–) is one of Jamaica's finest vocalists, with a wide repertoire from ska to lovers rock, but most famed for romantic songs like his 1974, number one, UK hit, "Everything I own".

Alton and Hortense Ellis – brother and sister Jamaican singers of ska, rocksteady and reggae; Alton (1938-2008) was one of the outstanding innovators of Jamaican music, with many hits and albums still available – *Sunday Coming* is one of the best; Hortense (1941-2006) recorded many singles for Studio One and Duke Reid.

p. 46.

Dutty tough – as hard as earth (dutty/dirt), from Akan *dote*, soil.

Ah wha'ppen to oonoo,/ah Coronation market u deh? – why are you sitting with your legs apart like a seller on Coronation market?

Jackie Edwards – (1938-1992), smooth singer in the Nat King Cole style and successful song writer who came to the UK in the 1960s and wrote for Island Records, including the Spencer Davis' number one hit, "Keep on Running".

Mortimo Planno – (1929-2006) Rastafarian mentor to Bob Marley and famous for controlling a huge crowd come to welcome the arrival of Haile Selassie at Kingston's airport in 1966.

p. 48.

Singerman, sing me a song – by the rocksteady group, The Kingstonians (1970).

Lancaster House – was formerly the location of the Colonial Office.

Federation – the abortive West Indies Federation which lasted only from 1958-1962, when Alexander Bustamente, who was anti-federalist, defeated the pro-federalist Norman Manley in a Jamaican referendum. With Jamaica's exit, Federation collapsed.

p. 49.

Studley Grange – a council building used by the community at 55, Louis Street in Chapeltown. A temporary building round the back was used by the sound systems. For the past eleven years it has been The Feel Good Factor, a community health centre.

Uhuru – (freedom, in Sahili) was a group of African Caribbean arts activists of the 1970s and 1980s. Annette Liburd was one of the first black teachers in Leeds; Violet Hendrickson designed carnival costumes; Imru Caesar (Bakari) published a collection of poems, *Secret Lives*, with Bogle L'Ouverture Publications in 1986.

Mpho – Mpho Ya Badimo, South African woman poet from Mafeking.

p. 51.

labrish – talk, gossip

kibba – shut her mouth, silence her.

p. 57.

du-rag – or doo rag, headscarf, usually black and tied at the back, mostly worn by men.

water-pumpy – a Jamaican dance; the body imitates the movements of pumping water – hear Johnny Osbourne's 1983 song, "Water Pumping".

sleng teng – fast dancehall style of music. Wayne Smith's King Jammy produced single, "Under Mi Sleng Teng" (1985) was the first computer generated track.

102

sing-jays – somewhere between singing and toasting (as a d-jay does), a style popularised by Michigan and Smiley and Eek-a-Mouse in the 1980s.

Dons – originally the leaders of Jamaican inner city ("garrison") communities who offered both protection and rough justice; from this came the dons and donettes of the dancehall.

p. 58.

Shabba Ranks, Tiger Man, Cutty Ranks and Ninja Man were all stars of the Jamaican dancehall or ragga, and the speeded-up, tongue-twisting dj style. There subjects were often gun-crime, ghetto dons, male boasting. There was much debate within middle-class Jamaica about whether this music just recorded actuality or celebrated and amplified criminality. If ganja and conscious (spiritual) lyrics were a significant element of roots reggae; slackness was the style, and cocaine the 1980s dancehall drug of choice.

twenty-one gun talk – both the celebration of guns, and the salutes made with fingers imitating guns by the crowd for the selector.

haul and pull it, selecta – the dancehall crowds' command to the selector to pick up the needle from the vinyl record track and return it to the beginning – i.e. it was a popular track for dancing. The *selecta* chose the records to play on the sound system, whilst the dj toasted/chanted over the instrumental track.

click suit – a fashionable style via the USA, early hip-hop, with big shirts and baggy trousers that found its way into the UK dancehall arena.

Travel Fox – were fashionable trainers of the 80s and 90s.

p. 59.

Sir Coxsone – Clement Dodd (1932-2004), the owner/producer of the Jamaican Studio One label, who recorded some of the best and most enduring ska, rocksteady and reggae in the 1960s, 70s and 80s.

Saxon – Saxon Studio International was a London-based sound system and record label, with a distinctively UK reggae style, featuring artists such as Papa Levi, Maxie Priest, Smiley Culture and Tippa Irie.

heartical – of the heart, righteous, conscious, Rastafarian influenced reggae (also a sound system of that name).

Tosh, D Brown, Jacob Miller – Peter Tosh (1944-1987), originally one of the Wailers, artist of political reggae in *Legalise It* (1976) and *Equal Rights* (1977), sadly murdered; Dennis Brown (1957-1999) originally a child star who bridged reggae, dancehall and lovers rock. "Money in My Pocket" was his biggest hit, the records he made with Winston Niney Holness posssibly the best; Jacob Miller (1952-1980) made albums on his own and as lead singer with Inner Circle. His greatest work was made with Augustus Pablo, sides such as "Who Say Jah No Dread".

Do you know what it means to have a revolution – is on Dennis Brown's compilation album *Love and Hate*.

Baron – a Manchester-based sound system of the 1980s.

Sparta and Maverick – Leeds-based sound systems.

King Tubby – Osbourne Ruddock (1941-1989), the sound engineer who took the art of taking apart and remixing reggae tracks to its highest, spaciest, mind-bending peak. *King Tubbys Meets Rockers Uptown* (1976) is probably his most famous album. Dub plates were one-off acetate discs whose exclusivity brought kudos to the sound system operator.

Jungle Warrior – a Leeds-based sound system.

p. 60.

beaver hats – wool velour hats popularised in the film *Rockers* (1978) – see images of Gregory Isaacs.

irie –feeling alright, feeling good – Rastafarian origins.

skanking – a kind of running-on-the-spot (fast as in ska; slow, easy skanking, as in reggae), elbows-up, fists clenched, style of dancing. Other variants included steppers and later rockers, both related to styles of Jamaican music.

lick wood – to hit the wall to signal that the selector should rewind.

p. 61.

KD Ranko (Kevin D'Costa), *Stylo* (Auslon Lawrence), *Clifford Irie* (Clifford Hughes), *Sweet Voice* (Michael Bent) and *Fluid Irie* (Richard Smith) – were all Leeds-based toaster/sing-jays performing with sound systems.

p. 62.

nuff tan tuddy – enough are calm, relaxed (stand steady)

satah – stay and relax

cork – ie full

p. 63.

Dancehall queen – the winner of women's dancing competition in the dancehall, both formal and informal, local and international – a place where women carved out space for themselves through athleticism, display, and fashion styles that outraged the respectable. The dancehall queen belonged both in Jamaica and the UK.

butterfly – a dance which involves the flexing in an out of bent knees, imitating wings.

mampi batty – a full, well-rounded backside, no doubt displayed in batty riders, very high cut shorts.

p. 64.

jazz-funk – mostly instrumental style of the 1970s and early 80s, popular in UK clubs, as played by musicians such as Herbie Hancock (*Headhunters*), Stanley Clarke and Lonnie Liston Smith. Al Di Meola's Latin influenced music was also popular.

p. 65.

sprats – boots, Jack Sprat brand.

p. 67.

Lovers rock – A form of reggae, influenced by American soul and r & b. Very much the product of the U.K. reggae scene, and popular from the late '70s and 80s amongst Black Britons. Lovers rock mixed the smooth sounds of Chicago and Philadelphia soul with reggae basslines and rhythms. Louisa Marks made one of the first lovers rock tracks with her 1975 single "Caught You in a Lie"; Janet Kay had a first success with "I Do Love You" and then a national UK number 2 hit with "Silly Games". Later, Jamaican roots-reggae singers, including John Holt, Gregory Isaacs, Dennis Brown, and Freddie McGregor, used the style to widen their audiences. Lovers rock maintained its popularity into the '90s.

Farah & Gabicci – respectively designer trousers and tops without which no clubber could impress.

Colt 45 – the brand of lager most popular with the clubbers.

natties – male partners (natty dreads, with natural hair).

snowballs – a concoction of advocaat and lemonade, once the height of sophistication.

I've been wanting you – from Janet Kay's number two hit, "Silly Games".

p. 69.

16-bar MC – a rapper (mic controller) who can create a 16-line (bar) rhyming rap.

in a cipher – rappers standing around the mic, taking a turn in sequence.

G-star – brand of clothing popular with rappers.

spittin' in a style – spitting (speaking) out the lyrics in a rapid style.

Jah knows! Wha gwaan! Blood! Easy my yout! – all sayings with roots in reggae and with Rastafarian associations. *Wha gwaan!* – what's happening, going on; *Blood!* Blood brother/one blood. They have been passed down the generations, and some have spread beyond the black community, but do those who use them really know what they once meant?

p. 70.

Where cold ground was my bed – Bob Marley, "Talking Blues".

David Oluwale – (1930-1969), a Nigerian who met his death at the hands of racist policemen in Leeds in 1969.

Olive Morris (1952-1979) – a London-based community leader, feminist, black activist and fighter for squatters' rights.

Mangrove 9 – refers to the trial in 1970 of nine black men and women on charges that included incitement to riot. The Mangrove was a cafe in Notting Hill, London, a meeting place for black activists, regularly raided by the police. The trial exposed police racism and the jury acquitted the nine of all the charges.

New Cross Fire – a house fire that killed 13 young black people in the New Cross district of London in 1981, in an area of racial tension and National Front activity. There was a big campaign protesting the apparent lack of interest of the police in investigating the possibility of racially motivated arson.

p. 72.

ginny heads – plaited Afro hairstyle, also known as guinea-rows.

p. 76.

John Holt – (1947-) a smooth, soulful Jamaican singer, most popular in the mid to late 1970s, with classic albums such as *Time is the Master* and *A Thousand Volts of John Holt*, both 1973.

p. 83.

bennu – a bird like a phoenix.

barakas – blessings.

Garnett Silk – (1966-1994), one of the revivers of conscious reggae in the late 1980s and early 90s, with tuneful melodies and a smooth sweet voice. "Hello Mama Africa" can be found on his album *Garnett Silk Reggae Max.*

p. 84.

single-bible – or sinkle-bible, aloe vera, used as a healing plant.

Ciboney – indigenous, but long vanished native American inhabitants of Cuba and Jamaica. There is some evidence of Ciboney/Taino pottery style surviving amongst the Maroons in Jamaica.

p. 85.

Mavado – David Brooks, younger generation Jamaican dancehall sing-jay. His "I'm on the Rock" is on the *Best of Mavado* album.

p. 86.

crocus bag – a hessian or burlap sack, often containing flour.

p. 89.

bissy – or bizzy, kola nut, containing caffeine.

p. 92.

duppy stories – ghost stories, duppies, spirits of West African origin.

ABOUT THE AUTHOR

Khadijah Ibrahiim was born in Leeds of Jamaican parentage. Hailed as one of Yorkshire's most prolific poets by BBC Radio, she has appeared alongside the likes of Linton Kwesi Johnson, Lemn Sissay and Benjamin Zephaniah. She is a literary activist, researcher, educator and Artistic Director of Leeds Young Authors. Educated at the University of Leeds, she has a BA Honours in Arabic and Middle Eastern studies and a MA in Theatre Studies. She featured in the F-Words project in 2007 and in 2010 she was one of the nine British and South African poets in the British Council's Verbalised tour. In 2013 she was amongst several poets invited to Buckingham Palace, where the Queen and Duke honoured the work of contemporary British poetry. Her writing has been supported through Inscribe, a national writer development project housed at Peepal Tree Press.

p. 96.

cowrie shells – used for divination within Yoruba worship of orishas.

maroon blood – Maroons, the runaway slaves in Jamaica who set up free communities, held off British soldiers and forced the British colonial authorities to cede a treaty which left them in peace.

Fante, Yoruba – two of the West African nations/ language groups from which Africans were transported to the New World, including the Caribbean. The Creole languages of the Caribbean have many loanwords from Fante (Akan). Yoruba peoples bequeathed the Caribbean such Orisha based religions as Santeria (Cuba) and Shango (Trinidad).

Oshun – Orisha/ river or sea goddess of the Yoruba pantheon associated with love, beauty and wealth.

green Dax – a hair wax made from beeswax and other natural oils.